The SHADOW WORK

The practice of discovering, awakening & integrating your shadow self.

A Prompted Journal

© Copyright 2022 - All rights reserved.

The content contained within this book may not be reproduced, duplicated or transmitted without direct written permission from the author or the publisher.

Under no circumstances will any blame or legal responsibility be held against the publisher, or author, for any damages, reparation, or monetary loss due to the information contained within this book. Either directly or indirectly. You are responsible for your own choices, actions, and results.

Legal Notice:

This book is copyright protected. This book is only for personal use. You cannot amend, distribute, sell, use, quote or paraphrase any part, or the content within this book, without the consent of the author or publisher.

Disclaimer Notice:

Please note the information contained within this document is for educational and entertainment purposes only. All effort has been executed to present accurate, up to date, and reliable, complete information. No warranties of any kind are declared or implied. Readers acknowledge that the author is not engaging in the rendering of legal, financial, medical or professional advice. The content within this book has been derived from various sources. Please consult a licensed professional before attempting any techniques outlined in this book.

By reading this document, the reader agrees that under no circumstances is the author responsible for any losses, direct or indirect, which are incurred as a result of the use of the information contained within this document, including, but not limited to, — errors, omissions, or inaccuracies.

INTUITIVE WAY
www.intuitive-way.com

Thank you for the purchase

Please take the time to leave a review so that others may know how they can enjoy this journal.

About the Author

My name is Tracy Addams, and I am a practicing witch from St. Petersburg, Florida.

I am 39 and I live with my two daughters and husband of 11 years. I am an artsy person who was always spiritually minded, but really took to occult studies as I travelled through Michoacán in Mexico when I was only 19. There I studied and practiced witchcraft near Teotihuacan and was initiated into the healing arts of tarot, herbalism, crystals, and Magick. I also volunteered in bio-intensive, organic farms, and love permaculture.

My story continued, as I migrated back to Los Angeles to work as a translator. Joining wicca covens, I was really inspired by other witches and what I didn't know. I eventually met my husband, who was also from Florida and I have been an independent witch for over 9 years.

This short journal is a welcome to you into the art of shadow work. I know you have found this book for a reason, and let me tell you I have the feeling you will be a completely different person when you finish it.

Forward

You are probably already hiding your shadow-self from others. You keep your shadow-self out of sight.

Your shadow aspects are not inherently negative and could actually even inspire creativity. Your shadow is a sub-conscious aspect of your personality that the ego does not identify with; that is, everything of which a person is not fully conscious is the shadow. The shadow is the unknown side, the 'darker' side of your personality. While the aspects of your personality that make up your shadow are usually perceived to be negative and dark, they can also be positive and uplifting! You may be extroverted, intuitive, or enjoy popularity. This can also be part of the shadow, but you see, these aren't 'negative' aspects. Again, through our youth we were taught to behave, to have manners, and to think rationally, and therefore what may be negative to one person is not negative to another.

Everyday shadow work refers to discovering these true shadow aspects, forgiving ourselves for having them, and healing from any traumas that may be associated with the sub-conscious. It is possible to understand your shadow for what it is--the unknown parts of yourself.

Looking into the shadow self requires self-observation.
Shadow aspects that you might possess include:

Anger Rage Envy Jealousy
Manipulative Exploitative Selfishness Self-Centeredness
Arrogance Egotistical Narcissistic Low Self-Esteem
Intolerant Prejudicial Defensive Stubborn

The sub-conscious mind is basically the shadow self, because we cannot see it clearly, and thus are not aware of it until we bring it into light. The conscious mind is basically light because it is what we perceive with our eyes and use to survive. Our shadow is the reason we do things in life unaware of why we do it.

With this in mind, shadow work can be very difficult to accomplish--rare are those who do it. Being vulnerable and honest is difficult, yes, but start today! As adults we should be able to handle life, but its sad how we repeat the same patterns thinking ourselves wise!

It is therefore important to realize that the shadow operates outside conscious awareness--but it isn't just negative and dark. It consists of gifts, potential, and talents, we just need to take those sub-conscious realities, and bring them into the light.

Contents

 THE BEST WAY TO DO SHADOW WORK

SHADOW WORK QUESTIONS

 SPOT YOUR SHADOW IN ACTION

INTEGRATE YOUR SHADOW

 OPEN NOTES FOR YOUR SHADOW WORK

The Best Way To Do Shadow Work

Shadow work starts by learning to have an inquisitive mind. Like prompting your Alexa, you prompt your shadow self with questions.

Questions will lead you into shadow work through the lens of introspection. What is this, you may ask? By asking yourself real questions that originate from long ago, you can analyze your way of thinking, and dig for truths that you don't particularly want to admit are true.

You won't want to uncover them yet, I know! As you find hidden gems in your potential though, you will want to continue.

Trust me, when you awaken your potential, life is magnificent.

Shadow work questions should accompany a journal, like this one. The journal is where you can return to again and again to dive deeply into your self.

All you need to do is turn to the open notes in this journal, or to any of the blank pages before and begin to study yourself with words.

The words get you thinking and, as you build your shadow work journal, your words will help you sort through your emotional shadow aspects. You will want to know where they come from, and what to do with yourself now that you have them identified.

Shadow is not all writing, it is observation--this includes meditation. As a walking meditation, observe yourself and pay attention to what you're feeling, why you're feeling this way, and where this feeling comes from. If it is really beneficial, you should write it down before you forget.

Shadow work comes while taking responsibility for the past, present and future. Just as a warning, you will also have to practice forgiveness with yourself. Be kind with yourself as you would others be kind to you.

Now, and later on, you will probably find out how empathy for yourself and others is very useful. This is how you will see yourself from new perspectives. When you release your shadow self from the subconscious, you will not only begin to be honest with yourself, but with the new you.

Shadow Work Questions

How to do shadow work?

While shadow work journals are all different, this one is full of questions. These questions are ultimately the best tools to use to get started. Once you have them finished, and I mean, this might take 6 months to a year, you will become an expert shadow worker, and you can go on to greater things.

Don't be doubtful, shadow work questions are how every shadow worker should begin. Of course, you might have already wondered if you are doing shadow work correctly or not? Shadow work questions are a wise way to confirm whether you have completed any shadow work yet or are just playing around.

Personally, I use shadow work questions to do shadow work, and I always will.

These journal questions will trigger old emotions, vivid memories and long lost experiences – often from childhood – that still sub-consciously affect you everyday. I do recommend you advance slowly, and keep your mind straight. This is a magickal journey of the spirit.

Don't worry, these questions will always encourage you to expand on your feelings. Any thoughts or stories that come up will be important! Where did this emotion of jealousy originate? How did this story of shame produce these toxic traits of low self-esteem? Now you know that to understand your thoughts, actions, and boundaries going forward will take persistence!

Some of the following shadow work questions will ask you about things you don't like. So the medication I prescribe is meditation, deep breathing and a tremendous amount of self-care! In order to process such memories, use your words and write in this journal. Write freely, there is no one to judge you here.

Shadow Work Questions

Have you ever felt wronged as a child?
In what way did you react?
Do you still act this way into adulthood?
Why?

Does betrayal play a part in your life?
What would you say to the person who betrayed you, or you betrayed?

Did youR mother or father ever let you down? How did you feel about it?

Is there an aspect of other people you wish you had in yourself?
Why don't you possess this quality already?

Have you ever found yourself over-thinking and having your mind racing?
Did you notice what caused this trigger?

Shadow Work Questions

Did your parents present themselves to you as people with core values?
Do you have core values today and do you model them from your parents?
Why or why not?

What do you hold most important to you?
Have you morals that you like to uphold in your actions and decisions?

If you ever felt envious of others, why did you feel this way?

What are the signs in your life that you are depressed, anxious, sad?

Are you often hard on yourself? Did you have a role model growing up you aspire to be like?
How do you handle high pressure situations? Are you ever kind to yourself on purpose?

Shadow Work Questions

You feel yourself getting angry, how do you act? What about your father, your mother, how do they react when angry? Did you get it from them?

Do you know what it means to be triggered? Where do you feel it first?

What does failure mean to you? If you fail how do you feel? Do you deny it, accept it, expect it? Do you feel shameful? What do your parents do when they fail?

How often do you have feelings of inadequacy? Do you ever feel stuck?

Do you have a relationship with your family? Are you the first, second, third born? What are the dynamics of the household?

Shadow Work Questions

Do you emulate your parents now? Do you see them in the way you are?
Does this make you feel good? Or do you still seek independence?

In what way do your parents exemplify poor behavior?
How do you feel knowing your parents aren't perfect and glorious?
Does your image of yourself include acceptance of poor behavior? In what way?

Do you have bad habits? How much of your life is occupied by bad habits?
Do you project these onto others?

You have a chance to improve yourself, would you? Why or why not?
Have you ever denied an opportunity that would have been good for you?
If yes, do you have feelings of regret?

Do you believe you are an exemplary human? A model citizen?

Shadow Work Questions

When you make a mistake do you forgive yourself?
Is there anything you do or have done that you deem to be unforgiveable?

Try to remember a time when you asked for forgiveness as a child. Did you receive forgiveness?

When you get what you want do you always want more? If things are going well do you fear them ending too soon?
Or, do you avoid making commitments because things are always too good to be true? Do you move from one place to another, from one relationship to another, one job to another?

If you are alone and bored what do you do? Can you rely on yourself to find joy?
What are your daily habits that you use to thrive?

Are there bills to pay, people to talk to, and work to do that you are avoiding, putting off, or completely ignoring?

Shadow Work Questions

If you are struck with negative emotions, are you still comfortable? Why can you OR can't you handle it?

Is there one person who you never want to forgive.
Do you hold this grudge and believe it is warranted?
Are you seeking justice and feeling pain at the same time?
What would it take to forgive them?

You have experienced trauma? How do you carry it? Where are you scars?

Did you handle your emotions well as a child? How about now, as an adult--do you handle your emotions? What has changed over time?

What kind of boundaries do you have now? Do you reinforce them? Who is allowed into your life? Is anyone allowed to come close?

Shadow Work Questions

Are you lying to yourself about something? How long have you been doing it?

Do you carry any bias against learning new things?
Can you think about new friends, family, neighbors without prejudice?

Does the divine feminine have a place in your life?

Do you have good feelings about the divine masculine?

How would you describe shadow work to your parents?

Shadow Work Questions

Make some goals with your shadow work. What are the three main parts of yourself you want to know more about?

What kind of hero did you look up to as a child? Do you still remember that feeling?

Do you remember being taught how to handle emotions as a child? What did you learn?

When you experience negative emotions now, how do you deal with them?

Have you ever hurt someone really badly? What did you do to them?

Shadow Work Questions

Do you regularly make promises and then break them? Do you enjoy making people cry?

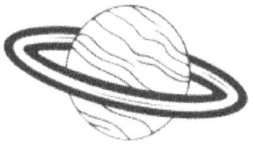

What do you deny about your life that you won't admit to be true?

What do you hide from others that you would be embarrassed about if they found?

How many lies did you tell this week? This month? This year?

Does lying make you feel good?

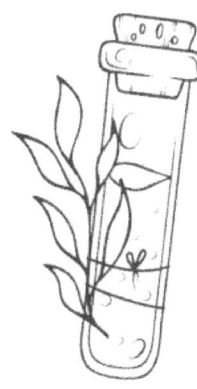

Shadow Work Questions

Have you ever purposefully tried to hurt yourself?

Have you thought about hurting someone else? Do you believe in self-defence or survival of the fittest?

How do move on in life when things are bad? Do you believe you or anyone should come to harm?

Do you remember when someone made a promise to you and broke it?
How do you feel about this promise? About this person?

Do you remember when you promised yourself something and broke it?
How you do you feel about the promise? About yourself?

Shadow Work Questions

Have you ever fallen out of love and had your heart broken?

Have you ever broken the heart of a loved one? Did you do so on purpose or by accident?

Do you find it easier to get by manipulating people with sex, lies, and denial?

Do you remember having questions as a child that you always wanted an answer to?
What is that question now?

Do you have a past event you want to talk to someone about?
Did they hurt you? Do they still plan to? Do you fear for your safety?

Shadow Work Questions

Explain the meaning of life in 100 words.

Do you often get into arguments? Do you avoid arguments? What was your last argument about?

If you feel a confrontation coming do you avoid it? Or do you get a thrill out of it?

Do you sometimes get physical reactions when your emotions run wild? What does it mean to you to lose your temper?

If you ran a self-care course what would you teach? Describe your perfect self-care activities.

Spot Your Shadow in Action

Every time you act out of your shadow, it gets bigger and bigger. However, let's not fuss, we now know the way to observe the shadow in action. What's important is to find the natural state of things--our innocence, and abide in it. When you do, you can extract from your shadow the goodness in instinct, emotion, and thought.

Here's how:

<u>Projections</u>

Many people *project* their issues onto others. Perhaps you do sometimes too. When you dislike something in someone, you might point it out in your mind--there! You've spotted the shadow of thought in action.

Please follow along.

Someone might **speak** with you, maybe in gossip, and project their shadow onto you. That happens too. Just remember, that that repressed anger, guilt, shame, and what they don't like about themselves — that's the same origin of your previous dislike thought. So, be the change you want to see. Instead of giving into that impulsive emotion they are trying to trigger in you, be careful of your projections and let it pass.

Pay attention to your self-image, and how you project yourself into your community. The world is complete with you, but you don't have to limit yourself to what others think of you. Eventually, your shadow work will reveal how people, places and things become mirrors through our daily life, and if we watch closely enough, we'll reflect who we really are in them.

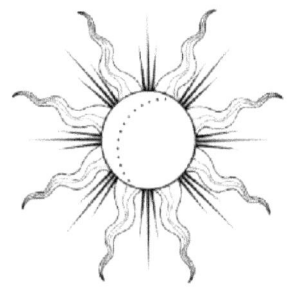

Spot Your Shadow in Action

<u>Triggers</u>

A trigger can be many things. Often it is formed during a trauma from our past. Essentially our brains are wired to chemically respond to stimuli, and old wiring just repeats itself over and over, unless we re-wire ourselves. We are wired with triggers that can be set off by a switch.

The shadow work allows us to study events that might cause conflicts in our lives without being triggered. This way, we can use the results of our shadow work to enable us to gather conscious pieces of our soul that are buried deep within us. And then, get them re-wired.

Pay attention and study your triggers without judgement! They are precisely the wounds you haven't healed from yet and your shadow self will reveal them to you. In fact, I suggest you enjoy healing as you catch your emotional triggers before you act them out. Honestly, you will be thankful you made a list of triggers and lined them up. When you do, you will be as brave as the blind, where your triggers no longer have power over you.

<u>Patterns</u>

As we discover patterns in our lives, certain aspects of our shadow will be revealed. The way to identify patterns is to practice a daily exercise before bed when you write down what you did that day! Like a film in your mind you can see what you did, what you said, and what you thought. Maybe you acted out, maybe your lost your temper, or gave up on someone you love. Who was in charge? You or your shadow?

Patterns and behaviors you repeat become sources of expression the shadow uses to mirror itself into your reality. The shadow desires to be seen but actually dislikes harmony, and will promote havoc.

The shadow wants you to become aware of itself but it is just mechanical in nature. It wants to be accepted but it is vanity and impermanence.

As you analyze your patterns of behavior you will discover aspects of your shadow self that will get bigger, stronger, and scarier. As you face different situations and you practice your shadow work you will find a breaking point when your shadow will lose its power over you and will cease to be intimidating. Then you are ready to start integrating your shadow.

Integrate Your Shadow

Integrating your shadow is done by reviewing your childhood again. It begins with the following questions:

Was I completely accepted as a child? *Yes? No? Sometimes?*
How did I feel most of the time? *Abused? Happy? Valued? Cared for? Nourished?*
Was I expected to behave a certain way? To please? To perform? *Were you reprimanded? Did you feel loved? Were you ever in trouble? Why or why didn't you love them back?*

Judging by your childhood experience you will find you had to form a shadow self to survive. This is where the root of the shadow self was formed. And this is why your shadow side is not wrong, it is just subconscious. Now I know you have already started, but I don't want you to jump too far ahead. Becoming aware of your shadow takes practice. Let's go on this journey together.

We are unaware of the shadow in the same way the blind can't recognize light and color. But we are going to use the power of conscious choice to observe and learn how to see our shadow self in action. Of course, the shadow work is designed as observe, judge, and reject negative aspects of our shadow self, so that we can reflect on it. Using a mirror image of our self we can live throughout our day and watch our shadow work progress.

When you find something negative, make peace with it and release it from the subconscious like a snake sheds its skin. If it's a positive aspect, reunite with it and be grateful as a mother nursing children.

The awareness we are building is illuminating the dawn of thought like a sunrise in the morning. This is how the shadow work is most important, in building awareness. Never give up! Shine a light on yourself or bring your shadow out of the darkness.

Your shadow self is unique to you, don't feel shame or consider yourself blamed. By ignoring it you know it will only get worse. Instead, do the shadow work and ignite fires of love, compassion, and acceptance.

Your shadow was born when you faced the prospect of becoming independent of your parents. It's natural, and everyone has a shadow. Antagonizing the shadow adds fuel to the fire of uncertainty. The shadow is your divine potential, so remark at its wonder and mystery. Love your shadow for the map it provides to rebuild your soul.

Integrate Your Shadow

Again we bring up triggers because we need to observe them everyday and even through the night. Triggers are like messengers and offer an invitation to delve deeper into unconscious parts of your shadow. From messengers you are given cues to the events that cause a reaction within you. Like dominos, one trigger will cause a chain reaction to many after it. So, keep looking until you find the original trigger. When you do you will see how they decreasingly have any effect on you.

This means that as you can step back from your emotional reaction--and simply observe it, instead of being controlled by it. This is a process of revealing the potential of your soul.

Unfortunately, triggers are loose connections within deep unresolved wounds of your soul. They need to be re-organized, managed, and absorbed into being again.

Shadow work is going to tempt you into judging whether the shadow is good or bad when you spot these triggers. Reserve your judgement and remain silent. Feel the wind around you and the earth beneath you. Let the fire burn inside you and the water of life nourish you. You have a harsh inner critic inside, so instead of rejecting your nature, let yourself tap into your innocence--your inner child--and be joyous in your shadow work.

Again, your shadow needs to be acknowledged. Fill it full of your attention and abide in its presence. Take command of your shadow with vigilance, and feel integrated with the work to handle it for the rest of your life.

Shadow work is the work of light amongst darkness. It is better to light one candle than to curse the darkness.

I PRAY YOU MAY FIND PEACE WITH YOUR SHADOW, AND BE SUCCESSFUL IN YOUR SHADOW WORK.

www.ingramcontent.com/pod-product-compliance
Lightning Source LLC
Chambersburg PA
CBHW081507080526
44589CB00017B/2677